Random Thoughts And Poems

by

Nadja

NadjaMedia.com

Nadja Media
530 Los Angeles Ave., Suite 115
Moorpark, California 93021

ISBN 10: 1-942057-0-59
ISBN 13: 978-1-942057-05-5

Copyright © 2014 by Nadja

All rights reserved. No part of this book may be reproduced by any mechanical, photographic, or electronic process, or in the form of a phonographic recording; nor may it be stored in a retrieval system, transmitted, or otherwise be copied for public or private use—other than for "fair use" as brief quotations embodied in articles and reviews—without prior written permission of the publisher.

The author of this book is not a doctor and does not dispense medical advice or prescribe the use of any technique as a form of treatment for physical, emotional, or medical problems without the advice of a physician, either directly or indirectly. If expert assistance or counseling is needed, the services of a competent professional should be sought. The intent of the author is only to offer information of a general nature to help you in your quest for emotional and spiritual well-being. In the event you use any of the information in this book for yourself, the author and publisher assume no responsibility for your actions. This is a work of fiction. Characters, places, and incidents are the product of the author's imagination and any resemblance to actual persons, living or dead, events, or localities is entirely coincidental.

Dedication

To all those people who are excited and inspired about waking up and participating in the renewal of Planet Earth, our Beloved Home.

— Nadja

Acknowledgments

With gratitude to have thoughts and feelings spill out in verse.

Introduction

Herein are forty-seven poems that run the gamut of human emotions from exuberance to deep insight. These inner monologues are meant to inspire and provide companionship. Nadja draws upon nature and the soul for her inspiration which is evident in her writing.

Contents

Travel	1
Intuitive Living	2
The Grand Opry	4
Benji's Song	8
Ocean Day	11
Color	13
Health	14
Awakening	21
Puma and Me	22
Health Nut	25
Seasons	28
Recovery and Discovery of Joy	31
The Hundredth Monkey	32

Light	33
Individual Path	35
Personal Politics	38
As Above So Below	40
Frequency	44
Genetic Creativity	45
The Golden Age	46
Self-Reliant	49
Holy Cow	53
Inner Life	54
Elevator	57
I AM	58
Universal Citizen	60
Guru	64
Hands	71

Eyes	72
Feet	73
Spine	74
Brain	75
My Heart	76
Prescription	77
Containers	78
Obstacle Course	81
The Body Sacred	82
Codes	84
Open Sesame	85
Calling Forth the Light	86
Reassurance	89
Unconscious Programming	90
Shift	92

Doing Nothing	93
Incarnation	94
Moonshine	95
The Great Turning	96
Final Words	98
Resources	99
About the Author	106
Also by Nadja	108

Travel

I'm going on vacation

It will not cost a thing

I'm going deep within my Self

What Joy this trip will bring

Intuitive Living

Give me an earthen home,

Sculpted by hands,

Beet kvass,

A garden,

Full view of earth and sky,

And I will cry tears of sheer joy

At the beauty of it all

Intuitive living

Summer, Spring

Winter, Fall

All day to paint,

Write, drum, dance, meditate

And at night commune

Intuitive Living

With the stars and moon

And dream of the Golden Age

That will be full upon us soon

The Grand Opry

Every day when I awake

The world is not the same

Oh, yay, it's wonderfully strange

'S no longer the same ol' game

Washed by frequencies

That go higher and higher

As they break down the old

And continue to inspire

A greater view

Of the life that we knew

And entry into

The life we desire

Every day when I awake

The Grand Opry

I'm getting stronger and stronger

Not the shadow of who I was

Oh, no, not any longer

I awake to who I AM

A soul complete

Who claims my Land

Unshakable, unstoppable

Made of rock and not of sand

Yet gentle as the morning rain

No more struggle

No more game

Living my life

Directing it all

The Grand Opry

No more stress

Having a ball

Just being me

My True Self

What a relief

The real wealth

I invite you to join me

In this growth

There's room enough

For us both

And many more

Around the globe

What a beautiful life

The Grand Opry

We have in store

From deep within

Our inner core

Come on now

Just open the door

Be who you are

And dance on the floor

Benji's Song

I met an Artist long ago

She was a beautiful, wise,

Loving, old, old Soul

She painted portraits

Of prostitutes left dead

By unconscious, very sick men

They were left like trash

To be disposed of

And never given thought to again

But Benji knew

They had as much of

The Creator within them

As you and I do

Benji's Song

She got their pictures

From the morgue

And gave them

Dignity, grace, and beauty

Through her portrait painting

Ever more

Benji has now passed away

The thought of her Work

Came back to me today

The love she gave

To the so-called

"Least of these"

Is a melody in my heart

Benji's Song

That continues to play and please

Knowing that this sensitive Soul

Applied her Art

And achieved her goal

In loving the Lost

And making them Whole

Benji, Darling,

Thank you for your song

You sang it well

And now you have returned

To the realms where you belong

Ocean Day

Ocean symphonies

Play for me

When I go down

To the edge of the sea

The waves lap the shore

With their sparkling white foam

Thank you, Seashore,

For sharing your home

I lay in the sun

And breathe in the mist

So many gifts

Too many to list:

The seagulls, the sand,

Ocean Day

The tide pools and more

Seaweed, driftwood,

And shells galore

I leave relaxed

And ready for life

Filled with calm

And emptied of strife

The music goes with me

Wherever I roam

Thank you, Seashore,

For sharing your home

Color

Color is magical

It vibrates and flows

All that it does for us

Nobody knows

Health

Something's growing in my body

It's definitely not from God

I'm looking for a Moses type

To heal it with his rod

Did this originate

From what I did

Or what I think?

What I eat

Or what I drink?

Health

Did it come from

Our poisoned planet

Or something else

That's present on it?

Every adversity brings a gift

What am I to learn from this?

What is it

I need to shift?

Health

Too self-absorbed

Too anti-social

Must I mingle

And be vocal

I'm so calm and peaceful

When I am alone

Comfortable and nourished

In my sacred space, my home

Health

Must I stretch my body

And my mind

Leave patterns wrought

Totally behind

Move into the heart

Process the fear and unwind

Sing, dance, drum,

Paint the Divine

Health

The personality is not

Who I am

I am a Pretender

Living on this Land

Truly I am a valiant Spirit

A warrior strong

Looking for where I fit

Where I belong

Health

Could it be I belong

Wherever I am

My body is my home

Is this the plan?

If so, I need to clean my house

Checking each detail

Scour every nook and cranny

Start clean without fail

Health

I want to be Authentic

I want to live True

So when this Work is done

I can totally merge with You

Awakening

I am feeling

I am healing

I am Soul

I am Whole

I am Earth

I am Sky

I am

The Universal Eye (I)

Puma and Me

The other day

In the wood

I saw a puma

On the path

So still it stood

Just looking at me

What a magnificent Being

Silhouetted against the sky

In total silence

The puma and I

Ears erect

Tail curled upward

From the ground

Puma and Me

What a treasure I had found

Puma symbolizes

Coming into your power

Speaking your Truth

Something I had lost

In my youth

Now is the time of rebirth

With this precious gift

From Mother Earth

Would it kill me

It sure could

Right then and there

In the darkening wood

Puma and Me

As I kept walking forward

It was as if

We both understood

That we were as One together

In our neighborhood

While I kept walking fearlessly

It bounded away so gracefully

What a moment in my history

Just myself with Puma

And Puma with me

Health Nut

Carrot juice, grains,

And dandelion stew

Raw nuts, seeds,

Sprouts, and fruit, too

Wow, I'm gettin' pure

As healthy as can be

Soon I can live

On just lungwort tea

Health Nut

I brush my skin

I walk in the dew

I massage my feet

And do yoga postures, too

I meditate daily

To clear my head

And follow all the rules

The Good Book said

Health Nut

I'm preparin' for the End

Whatever it will be

For I'm learnin' how to live

On just lungwort tea

Seasons

From Winter

To Spring

To Summer

To Fall

I love every season

I love them all

Winter is quiet

Covered with snow

Underneath all

Seeds are ready to grow

Spring brings forth flowers

Oh, what a show

Breathe in the colors

Seasons

That vibrate and glow

Summer offers berries

And fun in the sun

All kinds of veggies

And fruit by the ton

Fall colors leaves

Gives harvests to store

Pumpkins and potatoes

And seeds galore

Then comes Winter

And it all cycles again

It's been this way

Since the Beginning of When

Seasons

From Winter

To Spring

To Summer

To Fall

I love every season

I love them all

Recovery and Discovery of Joy

Deprogram yourself

Become the authentic person

You are

True to your core

No hiding anymore

From lemming to yearning

To learning to reviewing to redoing

To renewing to becoming

To freeing

To BEING

The Hundredth Monkey

I am the Hundredth Monkey

I've been gifted with the key

To first unlock myself

And thus Humanity

Light

The Light is so powerful

Filled with majesty and might

It infuses our bodies

To heal and delight

While melting the dross

To upgrade and renew

It's with us 24/7

Whoever knew

It is rarely seen

But does its magnificent Work

To free our True Being

Thank you Light

For all you do

Light

And most of all

For your keen insight

Individual Path

Observe but don't change

Through the muck and the slime

Through inhuman acts

To the Path Divine

A lily blooms

In its own time

The Pure is covered

By tons of debris

Trudging the Path

To set yourself Free

Whoever you are

Wherever you be

Keep trudging and traveling

Individual Path

Do the Deep Work

And you too will see

That Spark of God

That is placed deep within

No matter where or what you've been

You can help light the world

By shining your Light

To encourage others along

Out of the Dark Night

To uncover and discover

Their True Birthright

By growing and developing

What a grand sight

Individual Path

As the world becomes brighter

Light ignites Light

Personal Politics

We are responsible for what we think

Will you swim or will you sink

Our attitude is our altitude

It affects our health and others, too

Take charge of your mind

Tell it what you want it to do

Every day, each moment

We cast our vote

For which type of thought

We wish to promote

Will it be the negative or the positive

To rule our lives

Which one will it be

Personal Politics

To keep us in darkness

Or to set ourselves free?

As Above So Below

Behind closed doors

Beyond the sanitized life

Behind the eyes, the mouth, the words

Behind the ears, hearing, the brain

Volcanoes are ready to erupt

Floods are held back

Storms and monsoons of massive proportions

Are waiting for the signal of their keeper (us)

To explode and empty

To pave the way to authenticity

If ignored

They express themselves

As dis-ease, mental illness,

As Above So Below

Unimaginable chaos and cruelty

The subconscious mind

Was not permitted to participate

In the toxic Industrial Age

It was completely ignored

Those expressing it

Were locked away and medicated

Or celebrated as artists

Now is the time for mass catharsis

The healing of Humanity

Not by doctors

But by the People themselves

Once they have the key to unleashing

As Above So Below

Their subconscious mind and

A creative way to channel

Its potent wild energy out of their system

Through catharsis

They can fully embrace

Their Humanity and others

To arrive at Authenticity

And vibrant living in the Present

As totally alive sentient Beings

Mother Earth is leading the way

By doing her own cleansing

We, being her children,

Are following her example.

As Above So Below

The Kali Yuga is over at last

Spring is on the horizon

And we are blossoming

We will replenish the Earth

We will all heal

And peace will reign

On our most beautiful Planet

As above so below

Frequency

We are walking cell towers

Containers of frequency

What are you transmitting?

Beautiful thoughts like blooming flowers

Or fear, anger, and other dark powers?

Terrifying thunderstorms

Or gentle, healing spring showers?

Genetic Creativity

Our genes are not our masters

We tell them what to do

By what we believe

The thoughts we conceive

Negative or positive

To destroy or to renew

The Golden Age

I am part of you

The part of you with the Greater View

Encompassing the Height and the Depth

Of all you've done and all I knew

Come join me now

You're ready

For this ancient Vow

Has come to pass

We're ready to merge again

And grow to bloom once more at last

It's been an arduous journey

Step by step

Through centuries, lifetimes,

The Golden Age

Lifelines, and such

Living lots of flow

Unstuck and stuck

From flickering light and darkest muck

Our Time has come

Third dimension is now done

Connect your Heart and Soul as One

Your True Life has just begun

Dance, laugh, sing,

Be your Authentic Self and

Join the Fun

Unleashed, unedited, with total abandon

Step into the Light

The Golden Age

Of freedom, Freedom, FREEDOM

And Clear Loving Insight

Self-Reliant

We can be our own teachers

We can be our own counselors

We can be our own priests

We can be our own lovers

We can be our own best friends

We can do all this and still radiate love

To everyone and everything

We can do all this and still

Participate in the world

We can make our own medicine

Grow our own food

Heal ourselves of every malady

Design our own health program

Self-Reliant

Plumb our own depths to cleanse and heal

Build our own home

Be our own government

Travel anywhere without transportation

Create our own literature, music, movies,

clothes, paintings, dances

We can laugh uproariously and

Cry tears from the depths

We can change our frequency

To any level we wish

We can make ourselves visible or invisible

We can choose to speak or to not speak

We can communicate without words

Self-Reliant

We can decide to be abundant or

To experience lack

We are marvelously and miraculously made

Coming to Earth was our decision

We are powerful Beings

Who can live independently

Interdependently

We can manifest our own destiny

Stop looking outside yourself for help,

Answers, energy, inspiration, things

Be still

Go within

Connect with the Source of all Creation

Self-Reliant

Be in awe

Be in gratitude

Discover who you truly are

Come into your Total Beingness

Manifest, manifest, manifest

Your own destiny

Awaken

Live intuitively

Holy Cow

I am living in the NOW

Holy Cow

Holy Cow

I am living in the NOW

Holy Cow

I AM living in the Cow

Wholly NOW

Wholly NOW

I AM living in the Cow

Wholly NOW

Inner Life

I have a deep, rich

Very active inner life

Peopled with flowers

That sing and talk

Beautiful vistas

As well as

Tidal waves

Tsunamis

Volcanoes

And earthquakes

That crash into the consciousness

Animals and plants that speak

And play with me

Inner Life

Fairies, gnomes, elves,

Angels, and sylphs

That take me traveling

Colors so vibrant

That they enter my body

Like Liquid Light

And I'm not hungry for days

Music so exhilarating and rarified

That I am transformed and transported

Into the Realms of the Far Country

It's been a marvelous journey

When I am quiet and close my eyes

The curtain goes up

Inner Life

That's when the show begins

What an adventure

I should sell tickets

Move over, Hollywood.

Elevator

My Being is filled with

Portals, Doors,

Vortexes, and Gates

Slowly walk in

Press the button

For the top floor

Wow! Amazing

Never the same

I AM

To My Thetan

Thank you, thank you

For staying with me

Through this sojourn on Earth

Where I was blinded and could not see

Fumbling, stumbling everywhere

Trying to figure out

Who I was and how to Be

Wishing and begging to control and find

A way to master the reactive mind

Yet so focused on the task at hand

And all the distractions plentiful as sand

Who would know that I would grow

I AM

To learn to love and understand

That I truly am I AM

The joke's on me

I searched and searched

And took it way too seriously

So here I am, Dear Thetan,

I'm pleased to meet you

Yes, I AM

I AM, indeed, the Spirit Man

Universal Citizen

From little you to all in All

Your expanded Beingness

Amazingly wide and astonishingly tall

What a connection

To end the blindness

The imperfection

Always available

For those who dare

To take this path

Working through their pain and wrath

Letting go their story and past

To find their greatest treasure

Their Innermost wealth and riches

Universal Citizen

Way beyond all measure

Nothing now is hidden from you

You can heal yourself and renew

See the world through new eyes

When you finally Self-realize

To at last be truly wise

For you can view all

From a heightened perspective

Become one of humanity's elected

Qualified to teach and guide

Nothing left to cover or hide

By Universal Law abide

A Global Citizen

Universal Citizen

A Galactic Being

Able to See

And be Seen

Energized by the Central Sun

Your Higher Expression has begun

Exploring your multidimensionality

Which is part and parcel

Of the New Reality

Ready for a boatload of fun

Laughter and joy

Second to none

Living Whole

The prize is won

Universal Citizen

Through your hard, deep Work

You have become

A Free Being

A Universal Citizen

Guru

Are you searching

Are you seeking

To find a guru

The one who is perfect

And meant just for you

Look no further

Than your eyes or your nose

For your guru lies within you

Shhhh…Don't tell anyone

Because nobody knows

This is the Big Secret

That people ignore

They prefer to be blind

Guru

On their quest evermore

The Truth lies within them

This is the Good News

But to keep blinders on

This is what they choose

To do the Deep Work

They absolutely refuse

They believe it is easier

To give their power away

Than to clean up their cesspool

To observe what they think

To observe what they say

They are busy flying planes

Guru

All over the earth

To follow their leader

Whom they believe

Gave them true birth

Or they're desperately looking

In every cranny and nook

Praying to find

Just the right book

To tell them the truth

About who they are

Or to find the right teacher

They search near and far

When you finally stop looking

Guru

Give up and surrender

No longer a pretender

Be QUIET, go inside

Nothing left to hide

Do the Deep Work

Empty out

Still the mind

After this is completed

You will find

Your true guru

Who's patiently been waiting

Just for you

You were born a full package

Guru

With everything you need

Just like the oak

Grows from a seed

Open this Gift

Which you were given

To stop your seeking

And start livin'

Nurture this seed

Let it expand

Claim your birthright

And establish your land

A firm foundation

Is what you need

Guru

This you will have

Once you plant your seed

Grow a wonderful life

From roots deep in the ground

Develop strong branches

High above

Fill your heart

With gratitude and love

Then you can find

Your true Work and place

Become a positive Light

Doing your part

For the whole human race

Guru

With all the searching

You never knew

That you were indeed

Your perfect guru

The secret is out

Gee you are you (G-U-R-U)

Hands

My hands are

Made up of 10 servants

Waiting for my beck and call

To carry out my wishes

Every day of my journey

What wonderful tools

To enhance my life

And build my future

Thank you, hands,

My gratitude for you

Knows no bounds

Eyes

Eyes are the windows

Of the Soul

From them I can

Look out at the world

My mind and Soul interpret

How they see

Either through a glass darkly

Or Truth

Feet

My feet are my

Transport system

They enable me to

Move fast or slow

They are my structural foundation

When barefoot they plug me into

My Earth Mother

To complete my circuit

Spine

My spine is

My electrical wiring

Which orchestrates

The technology of my body

I must keep it supple

So it can do its best work

Unimpeded

Brain

My brain is the hard drive

Of my computer

My Soul can choose how to program it

What to override, delete, and create

The choice is a matter of frequency

And frequency depends on the degree

Of wakefulness

My Heart

My pump

My drum

My Connection

Prescription

Be still

And fill

Relax

Unwind

Love yourself

Be kind

Containers

We are containers of the Light

We are containers of the Divine

We are containers of Treasure

Way beyond the mind

We are containers of Joy

We are containers of Love

We are containers of Peace

Given from Above

Containers

Examine within

Watch with interest without

Know Thy Self

Then it will all work out

We are containers of the Light

We are containers of the Divine

We are containers of Treasure

Way beyond the mind

Containers

We are containers of Joy

We are containers of Love

We are containers of Peace

Given from Above

Obstacle Course

I am stepping up and over

The oppressing conformity

Of the herd

To my Truth

The Body Sacred

My body is filled with

Vortexes, codes, portals,

Doors, and gates

My heart is opening

This in turn opens my throat

To speak my Truth

My pineal is activated

And I See

My solar plexus

Is my sonar

My I Am

Is loving myself

Unconditionally

The Body Sacred

And so am I

My joy is broadcasted

To the world

Come join me

In this Work

Codes

Open the Book

Open the Words

Open the Letters

Open the thoughts

Open

Open Sesame

Go into Nature

Find the Portals

Enter

Absorb the templates

Open the Codes

Assimilate

Share

Calling Forth the Light

We call forth a column of Light

Pure Source Energy

Day and night

Vibrate, vibrate

Up and down

In and out

And all around

From the Heavens

Straight into the ground

Plug into the Circuit

Dance and sing

Out of the Box

Don't censor a thing

Calling Forth the Light

Music from the Spheres

It brings

Open your mouth

And let it Sing

Around the globe

It will ring

We see people

All over Earth

Joining in

And giving Birth

To the New

No longer old

Don't hold back

Calling Forth the Light

Just step on out

And be bold

Express who you truly are

A Magnificent Being

Born from a Star

Reassurance

Every Spring

The flowers

Reappear and grow

While rumors of wars and cataclysmic events

Continuously come and go

Drumming up tremendous fear

This seems to happen every year

Perhaps it has always been so

Gain perspective

Come to balance

Remember the flowers

The flowers

Know

Unconscious Programming

Remember when you

were at the top of the class

Excelling in all subjects, especially math

Beating the boys at their game

Outstanding on all sides

Absolutely no shame

Just living your life

The stakes were high

Always giving it your best

Enjoying each moment

Not wanting to rest

Until you eventually realize

That your culture sees you

Unconscious Programming

Through *their* eyes

As...

A...

Woman

In one glance

One breath

Herded together

Branded

Sanitized and

Standardized

Shift

Stop before you react

Wait before you reply

Try to see it differently

Through the other person's eye

Doing Nothing

A day doing nothing

Brings joy beyond belief

Being fully present

Just observing a leaf

Incarnation

With the end in sight

It was a remarkable chance

To test my mettle

So I could advance

Through each step of the journey

Wiser and stronger

No need to struggle

No, not any longer

Moonshine

The moon is so bright

On this mysterious night

The brightest it will be all year

There is no dark

The moon lights all

And there's nothing left to fear

The Great Turning

The Great Turning

Is turning us all

Inside out

Isn't this what

It's all about?

Each day is sparkling new

The past is past

At last we can be

Our own guru

Each day we turn the page

And fill it full

With vibrant life

No more bull

The Great Turning

The New Earth's here

Rejoice and Know

That we will heal

Flourish and grow

Final Words

"What lies behind us and what lies before us are tiny matters compared to what lies within us."

— Ralph Waldo Emerson

Resources

CenterForFoodSafety.org

FoodAndWaterWatch.org

Ienearth.org

FoodBabe.com

Mercola.com

NaturalNews.com

Bioneers.org

WestonPrice.org

NextWorldTV.com

Crimes Against Nature
by Robert F. Kennedy

Cosmic Ordering Made Easier
by Ellen Watts

Resources

M. T. Keshe

Patty Greer

Santos Bonacci

Dr. Masaru Emoto

Scott Werner, M.D.

Vandana Shiva

Jean Houston

Masanobu Fukuoka

Chunyi Lin

Susun Weed

Tusli Gabbard

John Hagelin, Ph.D

Paul Stamets

Resources

Buckmaster Fuller

David Wilcock

Matt Kahn

Lynn Waldrop

John Newton

Christel Hughes

Debora Wayne

Tarek Bibi

Lanna Spencer

Sophia Zoe

Jo Dunning

Lisa Transcendence Brown

Julie Renee

Resources

Eckhart Tolle

Neale Donald Walsch

Stacey Mayo

Dorian Light

Lottie Cooper

Andie DePass

Judy Cali

Marianne Williamson

Dr. Madlena Kantscheff

Dipal Shah

Jenny Ngo

Emmanuel Dagher

Magenta Pixie

Resources

Jarrad Hewett

Christine Day

Chief Golden Light Eagle

Janet Doerr

Karen LaGrange

Tamra Oviatt

Cathy Hohmeyer

Morry Zelcovitch

Rassouli

Akiane Kramarik

SARK

Shiloh Sophia

Aviva Gold

Resources

Ho'oponopono

The Emotion Code by Bradley Nelson

Emotional Freedom Technique (EFT)

Helpguide.org

Acim.org

Wopg.org

BirthingAndRebirthing.com

YouWealthRevolution.com

FromHeartacheToJoy.com

AcousticHealth.com

GalacticConnection.com

NotesFromTheUniverse.com

Homeopathic Cell Salts

Resources

OptimumHealthInstitute.com

NewPhoenixRising.com

CalixtoSuarez.com

Chanchka.com

Ringing Cedars.com

TED.com

Cohousing.org

Findhorn.org

Nature.org

GeoEngineeringWatch.org

iands.org

About the Author

After working many years in the public sector Nadja is reinventing herself as an artist and writer. She has an eclectic background. Her joys include adventuring on the Open Road, dancing, cooking, being in nature, writing and painting. She is also interested in natural building, organic gardening, alternative health, life-long learning, travel, and living moment to moment. Nadja writes for the conscious community and people who are interested in healing, meditation, transformation, ascension, and the New Earth. This includes highly sensitive people, Indigos, empaths, Light

Workers, energy healers, artists, visionaries, and those in recovery and discovery.

Also by Nadja

Soft-cover books, eBooks, MP3s, and CDs Smashwords, Amazon, Kindle, CreateSpace, CDBaby, iTunes, YouTube, and your local bookstore by request.

River of Living Light

Evolution Revolution

Random Thoughts and Poems

Hopi Blue Corn

El Maiz Azul de los Hopis

Visionary Tales for the New Earth

Color Me Bright Coloring Book

Blue Sky

Ascension Codes

Raps, Chants, and Rants

Women's Power Awakened

Ozzengoggle Poems

From the City of Shem

You Are Not Alone

Family Secrets

Flying Heart

Bullies

www.ingramcontent.com/pod-product-compliance
Lightning Source LLC
Chambersburg PA
CBHW070618050426
42450CB00011B/3076